The Book of Echoes

The Book of Echoes
David Gregory Welch

JACKLEG PRESS

JackLeg Press
www.jacklegpress.org

ISBN: 978-1956907230

Library of Congress Control Number: 2024945781
Cover design: Danika Isdahl
Cover art: *Six circular designs* (1878–1938) painting in high resolution by Richard Roland Holst. Original from the Rijksmuseum.

Also By David Gregory Welch

Everyone Who Is Dead

Praise for The Book of Echoes

The Book of Echoes is a tour de force of the internal voice, one that's sent out into the world and comes back in myriad waves, demonstrating the complicated, beautiful, and varied nature of the human mind. Taking on the voice of Robert Creeley, David Gregory Welch asks: "these / days what isn't / a religion?" and these poems answer that question time and time again: what we might seek from the outside world can also be found within the striations of the self, "a heart / full of wet sand // beating beside the ocean."
—Adam Clay, author of *Circle Back*

The Book of Echoes is a song not easily sung. "I'm alive and live in my failure to live," David Gregory Welch writes, the imperative clanging against his deft and lyrical restraint. Through captivating accounts of Tourette syndrome, Welch's language mirrors repeated movements and sounds, embodying Auden's vision of poetry as "a way of happening, a mouth." "Look," he writes, "I cannot move the way you hope I do, a blanket / in the breeze of its own control." David Welch's poems celebrate and transform the body's limits in this intoxicating, unforgettable collection.
—Jenny Molberg, author of *The Court of No Record*

Echoes are born of depth and dimension, in cavernous, resonant, and hard spaces. *The Book of Echoes* makes that kind of space: deep and expansive, rich and complex. Within it, David Gregory Welch's surreal poems ricochet and careen. They startle and rivet. Biting in its politics, singular in its observations, heartfelt in its confessions, his is a voice that resonates and lingers so that long after the reading is done, the poems remain and remain and remain.
—Jaswinder Bolina, author of *English as a Second Language and Other Poems*

Contents

For Justine

§

Ventriloquy

Let's play a game. It's called

EVERYONE APPLAUDS WHEN YOU DON'T
OPEN YOUR MOUTH. Never let them see

you say what you are
thinking. Never let them

determine which hand slips
inside the body, which seduces them

from the body they aren't meant to be
watching. Listen,

dummy: the jaw, like the heart, is a simple machine.

You have your whole life to hear
your voice

and wish it came
from somewhere else.

§

The Book of Echoes

In the Book of his music the corners have straightened
        and the day is bright gray turning green,
slow kisses on the eyelids of the sea

I strain to gather my absurdities

*

My babies parade waving their innocent flags

                as the bulbs burn phosphorescent, white,
opulent, sinister, and cold,

bouncing a red rubber ball in the veins

*

I too am reading the technical journals, but
first may we read about all those radio waves
racing down the blue lugubrious rainways

*

The indexed Webster Unabridged Dictionary—
the romance of it all was overwhelming

Put away your hair   Books shall speak to us

of Marilyn Monroe, her white teeth white—

Into the vast closed air of the slow

                    cherrywood romances of rainy cobblestones

my babies parade waving their innocent flags

*

             aching in rhythm to that pounding morning rain

We may read about all those radio waves

      & who dumbly begs a key   & who cannot pay his way
on the 15th day of November in the year of the motorcar

*

Elvis Peering-Eye danced with Carol Clifford, high,

seven thousand feet over one green schoolboy summer

Andy Butt was drunk in the Parthenon

*

Do you want me to take off my dress?

*

In a rare, unconscious moment,
it is such a good thing to be in love with you

And then one morning to waken perfect-faced
                in the square, on the farm, in my white block of hair

                        The most elegant present I could get
and I find my hand grows stale at the throttle

*

                        You can make this swooped transition on your lips
to be printed in simple type on old brown paper

*

It is night   You are asleep   And beautiful tears

sleep half sleep half silence and with reasons

*

Daughters prefer to lay 'em on a log and tear their hair

wan as pale thighs making apple belly strides

*

        Not me   I like to beat people up

*

                My hands make love to my body when my arms are around you
The most elegant present I could get!

*

Each tree stands alone in stillness

                         The withered leaves fly higher than dolls can see
I strain to gather my absurdities into a symbol

*

The cherrywood romances of rainy cobblestones

                              The dirt-covered ground, tied together

                   only with fifteen pieces

of glass on the roof of my tree

*

Whatever is going to happen is already happening

          is not genuine   it shines forth from their faces
                         will not kneel   for everything comes to it

Like Word Origins   and cribbage boards   or dreams

*

White boats   green planks   black dust   Atremble

The withered leaves fly higher than dolls can see

                   That the angels have supereminent wisdom is shown

and takes the eye away from the gray words

An Organ-Grinder's monkey does his dance
defying natural law, saying, "Go Fuck Yourselves,"

*

                      and I fall on my knees

*

Rivers of annoyance undermine the arrangements

*

         I am closing my window   Tears silence the wind

and the rust on the bolt in my door
which owe presence to our sleeping hands

*

                   These sonnets are an homage to myself

*

The logic of grammar is not genuine   it shines forth
The academy of the future is opening its doors

*

                How strange to be gone in a minute!

       White lakes tremble down to green goings on

Whatever is going to happen is already happening

*

I walk out in the bleak village and look for you

Georges Gilles de la Tourette

I gave my name
    to a locust   thrashing
inside the throat,
    & though I

wanted to open
    the skull & stitch
I could not   though
    I wanted

to tame   like a hypnotist,
    the phantoms
rising   I left only
    my name

a tourniquet
    cursed around
the holy   trinity
    of my blood,

its ghost   the tongue
    you lay out
to display pale
    liquid,

a banquet hall,
    this small red bell
being beaten at
    its center

Echolalia

As to impose one part
      of a pattern

            onto another

as if firsts & lasts were one
      & the same.

          As if the moon

could haul through you
      as yolk, waving

          from our bodies'

heat. As if firsts & lasts
      were one & the same.

          As we are so

wonderfully done
      with each other.

          As yolk, waving

from our bodies' heat.
        As a yell able

                to outyell itself

as we are so wonderfully
        done with each other.

                As I

inhale the impalpable
        breezes that set in

                upon me

as a yell able to outyell
        itself. As if the sky

                itself had

been snowed upon.
        As I inhale

                the impalpable

breezes that set in
        upon me,

                as I wander

in a dream through
      your dream

           as if the sky

itself had been snowed upon.
      As a flower,

        as a fire,

as a hushed footfall.
      As I wander

         in a dream

through your dream
      as my own.

         Prick my ears,

Lord. Make them hungry
      as a flower,

        as a fire,

as a hushed footfall.
      As if the trees

         by their very roots

had hold of us. As my own,
`   prick my ears,

                Lord. Make them

hungry as if the moon
           could haul

                through you.

As if the trees
           by their very roots

                had hold of us

as to impose one part
           of a pattern

                onto another.

Instructional Ghazal

1: on lying

You will want to make the corners of the mouth
very dark, so the teeth appear asleep and silent inside the mouth.

2: on breathing

Even coming softly the wind rattles the sills.
The windows whistle a song in parting, like the mouth.

3: on swallowing

Take only the smallest bodies with your tongue: accept
the muscled rules you must maintain inside the mouth.

4: on kissing

I felt your nose like a plum in the dark. Suddenly
I was swimming—unable to breathe or see the mouth.

5: on tying

There are three ways you can teethe and three
knots: the shoelace, the noose, and the mouth.

6: on loving

If his stomach is the surest path to a man's heart,
you must be sure to take him by the mouth.

7: on closing

In spite of tradition, I'm leaving it open:
[place any name you want in my mouth]

Prodrome

A thought enters
your head. It imagines itself

growing like an infant.

How wonderful it is to be born!
How lovely & unrepentant

it is to live.

You must remember that
also there is love tended

to thrive against the frost.

(I, too, numb to apples rotting
against the ground.)

What's important now is we

recover
our senses.

Echopraxia

I pull a rabbit
    from my tongue
& place it
    on the wall   pinning
its shadow back
    like a shawl

lamplit   little ghost
    my hands
unfold their trick
    of keeping
the river in the air
    moving until

a field of turbines
    spreads their dull
arms above the dam
    one senses in
the stomach's pit
    The rabbit

spreads   bare
    its fur pillowed
across the floor
    When I reach
inside the glove
    of its skull

my fingers curl
    into its teeth
I bear them down
    The arms wave on
above the field   whitely
    humming

Tourette's as Thanks for Everything You Can Put in Your Mouth

A word, for instance, or what you know in another's mouth would be a word you've not yet known.

Bite your tongue.

You do not speak in it or others; but you know it speaks

for you—know to thank it, even as it's always searching.

You let it touch the roof, a hammer
        unhinging weakness.

What comes across without surprise first

appears otherwise: sweet sound or light leaning,

greenly against the leaves. Leave it, we say when a dog steals the world, when it wants it, like a wish,

into its mouth. What else is thanks

but a wish the body no longer needs to wish? What else to say

once the body calms? Leave it.

Tourette Syndrome

I do not ask

        by any means

                to be more

human

        I do not

                by any means

ask for means

        beyond means

                Bodies rise

to definition

        by fact

                of definition—

always there

        are hours

                which are

not ours

        of which to

                speak

Variations on a Theme by Breton

My body of light and my body of steam.

My body of light lavender and blood.

My body of blue lights flashing on a plane's wing.

With the body of relent.

My body without.

My body with circumstance and of a good tongue of storm.

With the signature bent of a spasming host.

My body with the back of a body fleeing vertically, with a body of quicksilver, with a back of light.

This body a curvature and dampened hearth.

My body of doing.

My body with the body of smoke, with a body of tongue and the body of split wood wrested from rain.

This body of the evidence of love.

My body my body stiff with a body of what has been.

A body with the body of the broken sea.
My body alone and the body of false memory of the body of love.

My body with the body of wood always under the axe.

My body with the body of water level of level of air and light and the drop of a glass
   where one has just been drinking.

My body not unlike the body that is.

Tourette's as Bildungsroman

"There is no end in is,"
Bidart writes, beginning

in the imagination of indefinite
permanence. Imperfection

lists, a lilting lesson
in how to stretch each year

in spirit, a perpetuation
of motion as means

separated from its ends.
To curse in rapture is the same

whether the body is beguiled
or bare. There is no moral

there. Whatever *is* in Is is only
offered after its end.

§

Self-Portrait as Horizon

The first time I saw the ocean I slipped into it
fully clothed   My eyes: twin oysters gleaming in their nacre

Nude, each morning the sun
                                        places a bowl of salt in my mouth

An aphrodisiac: the slow rise of what returns,

                                                        of what turns
just out of reach   Still my skin swells through thirst

Though I know you always look to me, I'm not so foolish
to think myself the end of the line   I am always distant,

always letting my dark slip
                                        peek out in the worst weather

To keep the smooth curve of my side,
where would that get you?   To know the pull

                                                        of the tides,
pass the heron turning
                toward the distant islands…

Look   I cannot move the way you hope I do, a blanket
in the breeze of its own control

I am only what you can touch of smoke:

                              the fading bather looking,

finally, to return to the sea

Cesarean

My brothers and sisters each died before
any could meet my father. I was taken from my mother
by forceps after fourteen hours. One thing
everyone has in common: a merciful failure
to remember the moment of their birth. My brain misfires.
My spine is curved. I'm missing a muscle above my heart.
My grandmother's father died from pneumonia,
a complication of his broken back. I'm afraid
if I have children, I'll pass on only what I lack.
My father's father never knew his father,
whose widow died in a kitchen fire.
I'm alive and live in my failure to live.
This morning, I read Caesar entered the world
by the same instrument that took him from it.

Dear Hell

I'm most successful in my disappointments.
I've wanted and tried to let go
of everyone who has shown me kindness.
Never mind life. It's a *love* everlasting
that's so slow going. In a basement apartment
ten blocks away, K.'s mind smolders, sour
in the thought of how long our given distance
will stay with us. As for me, I am intact, Rimbaud
wrote, secure in his sickness. Hedge toward honesty
and you're shown the door. That's one way
to see how someone predisposed to seeing
Hell might approach our present situation.
But *you* know that. You burrow, inexact in my thinking,
while I sputter to even use my body for a living.

You Meet Someone and Later You Meet Their Dancing and You Have to Start Again

You meet someone and inside of them
you know there swells
a small country brimming
with steel and beasts of labor.
You love the country
and so you fear it.
Its flora fascinates you.
You wish to visit, though
you worry you won't
wear the right clothes, that you'll fail
to order a drink, ask directions,
assure the clerk in the flower
shop you aren't a thief.
They're only roses. They remind you
of the one you love.
Even with your eyes closed
in your own mouth you'd know
they're roses.

Heirlooms

You can hear them becoming quiet,
which they must, in order to haunt your thoughts
with worry about whether you locked the front door
or left the window unlatched beside your jewelry box,
the ring you insist you'll soon insure hidden
exactly where you know it must be found. Your grandmother,
were she alive, would never forgive you. Years ago
she met the thieves and lived to never tell you
about it, family lore silent as a marriage
left alone too long. There is no greater noise.
It swells for years inside the head, a quartet of wind
instruments distancing your fear, as all the while
the thieves gather what they came for, each moment
uncovered to reveal the next living inside it.

Reservoirs

The apple was not an apple when the rains came
The grave spurned the groundskeeper's shovel when the rains came

No sacrament   no scripture   There were no reservoirs
save an ark beneath the steeple when the rains came

First the river wouldn't fill   Then the valley's hills
rose like the back of a camel when the rains came

The piano pursed its mouth of strings   The tenor kissed
his weathered hymnal when the rains came

There was no weathered landscape   there were neither
the hanging gardens nor Babel when the rains came

Lying on his back   the shepherd fanned his arms and legs
No one told him he could not impress an angel when the rains came

"our glosses / wanting in this world" *"Can you remember?"*
My name in Hebrew means Beloved or   blissful when the rains came

Wild Asparagus

Eating something in order to identify it is not
the smartest thing I've ever done.
I am always on the run—*That's nature.*
It's my most distinguishing feature.
I work. I learn. I twitch through
my wits. Take imagination for instance:

it's stricken by fits—*And fights of fancy*—
to spats of speaking itself aloud.
It's that man in stripes and a stocking cap—
Always hoping to be standing
and discovered lonely in a crowd.
But when we take ourselves aback,

we turn to discover the world
with our mouths. That's how such poison
comes—*Like a dog.* It sings to itself.
It hums. *It laps at the groundwater*
with a soft but fearless tongue. Then it sleeps
with open eyes—*In case it needs to run.*

Study for Two Swans

1.

The necks and heads
of two swans,
tipped down
so the upper breadths
of their bills touch
at the tips, approximate
the shape of
a bottomless heart.

2.

Introduced to
a lake, two swans
may move
to make more
swans, though
the lake takes
no part in it.

3.

In my arms,
one swan is looking
for another swan.
It's a small swan.

If nothing else
may my arms
be small
shores for swans.

4.

So two swans are like
two hearts: if one is empty
the other empties.

5.

If you see no swans,
you see something
else, but if you see
nothing else
you see two swans.

6.

Two swans are still two
lovers. Look!—now our feathers
are getting dirty.

7.

You may do this
with your arms—

encircle them behind
your back to
embrace
a second body.

But you cannot turn
a single thing into swans.

Love Song

That each for the other should be
the hero, & love what failure falls

as dusk, alighting across what brightness seems
                                    otherwise easily seen.

Valentine

Whether water offers us
its memory of what was
once willed inside it,

whether one molecule
remembers the hand
that holds the glass,

another the arm that bends it
toward the kiss, two more

the lips, which part
to leave such room
for love: whether water dissolves
any one molecule

of love, let ours be always
remembered as we found it.

A Language or Barrier of Love
a translation for Jack Spicer

The nose is a simple machine

we learn to speak under

An Economics

Wind against the trees, and then the cause of the hunger
was determined. You imagined it sitting in the car,
the posterity of a broken seatbelt slung over its shoulder,
hands on the steering wheel without money
for gas, how the eye sees one thing and the fingertip
touches another. A cause, a hunger. An exchange
of directions. The face's first touch in a year
extending from the hands of a doctor. A wind against the trees.
Leaves, halfway to hands already, reddened by the end of their work
in autumn. Skin: an economics of water and wind. The trees evergreen.
The trees otherwise. So it ends. It ends. It begins.

Upper Peninsula

I should be there
Among the daffodils
After we arrive
Our trains turn into
Their ghosts behind us
I'm trying to imagine how
To not carry my breasts
In front of you
I am trying to
Reason with that
Bat I keep hearing here
But cannot see
I have always loved
The word *proboscis*
In that I've been successful
The northern wind
Moves like a pike
Beneath this evergreen
I cannot see
I keep hearing
Is it yet summer
Where you are too

As for Names

Some are Johns. Or Janes, as some come to see
when sussing out their nouns. Their names.
Tags weary. They hang. There may be something
newly dreary then. As when a hen sends her beak
along to squawk about the maw—a half-cocked yawn—
That's being fresh. Some days all day is lost

in game. John begins to wax
and wanes the night—*So light!*—away with Jane.
Sex breeds turns. It spurns. A new sheen of wax.
And so up soften some whips, some soap.
Then hope about what stirs. A hex
makes way to John, then Jane, then throughout

the day there's always some soft coming stir.
Shift. Quick. A listing like an itch
wilting behind the hilt. Guilt never comes
slow toward what's not done. It runs. The chest
brims—*Such skin!*—always for what it is: a teat. Neither
hand nor anything appearing below it. But then again.

Passages

a translation for Jack Spicer

with the letters of
the alphabet
spell what you
are hearing

at the moment of
your death the words
are correctly spelled

as if your heart
will ever let
you hear the
moment it breaks

Postscript for the Beginning

a translation for Jack Spicer

No one knows exactly the manner of fish swimming
though we're all jealous little voyeurs
so we watch them.

We tour their homes and the fish remain cool to it.
They close their eyes. Imagine a heart
full of wet sand

beating beside the ocean. Now crawl out of bed
and touch your toes.
The cloudy movements!

The humpbacked mountains!

Reverse Ghazal

As if intensity were a virtue we say good and.
As if plenty weren't enough we still ask for a name.

As if sea and water. As there is a difference.
One hand holding what the other forgets.

As if breeze against its neck suggests
the owl hasn't time to turn a second chance.

As if "revise," "revamp," "reinvent." (Thus I
ask you come tamp down the past.)

As if only "If" can have its way with things.
O, let me lay down beside you. Tie my tongue.

As if: Apostrophe of wheat, I cannot thresh You.
Your eye holds my hand like a scythe.

As if weep as if cry out because a name
stays locks as if your tooth were a key.

As if intensely a virtue we say O,
let me lay my tongue down. Let me lie.

As if please. Come nuzzle me, stranger—
here are my hands, are my hands, are my hands.

The Ongoing Always Goes Back

On incompleteness much can't be said—
each sentence slants. Then a chance to stand
behind the two-way glass of what you know
shines back—*A dim light moves.* That's fine.
O.K. How do you choose
yourself each day? A dress.

A hat. An evening feeling of coming back
to what you know—*That's home.*
Sometimes the mind winds like a scarf.
A little woven work of art! Don't get smart.
Let's get back to what we hear—
"above us the moon remains unclear."

That's all you do: look to what's hung
over you—*It's called oversight*—a moth
repairing to light to look
for what's behind what's bright…

                    "Evening unfolds
like a map," the moth cries, "Don't forget the write!"
"But I ain't going nowhere," says the light.

§

The Course of Human History Personified

There you are.
You are discovering them.
And they you. So the world
so discomfits. As though
each side of the safari sets out
opposite one violent viewing.
Blood blooms beneath the brain.
Arrows arrest the loveliest
animal, autumn
arrests the rest of our affections.

At last the scene becomes another
star acting against loneliness. Ignited
in pitch the trumpet flares
such muted alarm.

I Doubt They Would Notice the Mustachioed Man's Wife

How you carry yourself in
the train station says a lot
about the Constitution   what
it lets you experience in
the eyes of the engineers
and how one day you may
believe it necessary to board
the express out of town
you tell no one   and in this
you take your freedom
you take a cold sandwich
from the thin man pushing
his cart down the aisle   outside
the trees impress the darkness
of the train as you pass
into the middle of America
so much change rattles
around in your head you know
you cannot sleep   you
know sleep is for those
on slower land   around their heads
it is morning   the alarms
have yet to sound   this pleases
you   the trains are moving swiftly
at their destinations

What's It To You

Inside of Town Hall the townspeople are
having a meeting. What's it to you, one of them asks
as I walk in and I say very little, smiling as they imagine
whether I mean what I say. Sitting in the corner
I see a voluminously arresting fruit plate. It's brimming
with papaya, which I thought was out of season.
Mangos, too. And something that resembles eggs
but is not eggs. The Egg Problem is currently
under discussion. Tom of course brought it to the table,
and Frank thought it best to let it go, but you know
how these things go. In the Town Hall courtyard,
the egg trees continue their yields against reason.
The smell is confusing. Labradors lean their ears
into the wind, sniffing as the scent of the egg trees
pauses against their wet nostrils. The town dogs
are healthy, which is the most certain sign of prosperity
we've had in a long time. It means a lot to all of us.
All summer the egg trees have tempted men
and women alike with their tapered shapes.
Tom doesn't think we should stand for it.
Tom doesn't really know what he is talking about
is the gist of Frank's rebuttal. I tend to agree.
The light is very low. The coffee is of course terrible
and someone asks why these meetings always resemble
pancake breakfasts held in the basement of a church.
I think he means it more in spirit. The eggs remain unbroken
in their shells. Then Sarah makes an arresting contribution.
Papayas are an aphrodisiac. Mangos, too.

Thanks for Sending Tom Jones to My Door in a Box

He wouldn't leave.

All night we watched through the slats in the blinds
and he just sat there, sullen.

We're told of *sexual escapades*,

that he's *amorous, high-spirited*. The evidence is curious.
Though once, his compact body opened,

the dusty musk perfuming

the air, briefly, and we watched
as he clapped himself around the quickening breeze.

It was cold out, and April,

his thin skin marked up like a ledger,
beige, a bit torn.

We argued for hours

over whether to take him in,
offer cigarettes or an orange,

a change of clothes;

whether to call the authorities or take care of him ourselves.
        The slim cuts on our hands became their own story.

        A possum limped about the lawn

as the skyline crept purple.
        And somewhere, the leaves shook their veracity,

                as when in spring scents rise

and fade with quickened ease. As when a body is paper
        it sits there, believing the fluttering wind.

Frog

a translation for Jack Spicer

I like the novels
that make me come

like a frog

into poolwater
or the particular green leaf

that heaven remembers of happiness.
You can still breathe in

through your own nose

though your heart is full of water.
You can smell the single black smoke of a pinefire.

The black forest above a bed of single green needles.

The Ladder

You look at the ladder leaning against
the tree where the bear sits hidden
amongst the crown of branches. You know
you can reach the bear. & you know, too,
the bear is dying of loneliness. You can see yourself
climbing rung by rung until you enter the green
sea of leaves above where the trunk begins
to thin, can see your legs wrapping against the bark
as your hands reach for surer holds. You
could climb higher above yourself
& remember how you spent your childhood
in trees like this, though you never had to
brave bears, fire, winds blowing in across the country
only to pass by whatever they touch.
That the bear is lonely is unimpeachable,
a sort of word you know must be connected
to a tree. You think of the bear hiding there & want
to holler at him, or her. The thicket of fur guarding
such willful paws, the sad eyes you know best
bred only in bears, who sleep with their sadness
buried inside them all winter. This must be,
after all, why the bear is hiding there.
& that's when it dawns on you: you're still
standing against the ground, the ladder rising
in front of you like a long winter,
& above it the warm breadth of the bear
breathing against the leaves, its body full
of everything you've yet to see.

Nevermind the Lightning

That's a waltz in your mouth,
said the dentist. Don't you light that
in here—we can't all keep time
with our tongues like that. It isn't fair.
The tooth said, So what should I do?
And the mouth said,
Stay here. And the bridge
on the eastern shore creaked
as it shook a bit in the wind.

*

The dentist said, I built a bridge.
Don't eat anything
larger than a tooth for a week.
The mouth asked, Which tooth?
You can choose, the dentist said.
Out east, said the mouth,
they have lobsters as small as molars.
So you can eat lobster, the dentist said.
If I choose to, said the mouth.

*

Said the tooth to the wind—
I'm not without my sympathies
for your loneliness.

64

In the mouth, my only
company is the tongue,
which constantly wanders. I said
wonders, the wind said—
the sky is a mouth
where the hawk-tongue wonders.

*

When the dentist introduced
the drill to the tooth,
he allowed a small wind
to settle in, burrowing into
the molar like a mole.
Everything must have a home,
the dentist said. Yes, said the mouth.
I understand. Especially the wind,
which is hollow like a tooth.

*

The wind, the mouth said, is
a sort of waltz. It loses a step
every third season.
But a waltz takes a step back
every second season. So
a waltz is a sort of tongue,
licking back over itself
when it's done. I can't
see that, the wind said. I can

*

see what you're saying,
the mouth said. It frightens me.
I'm not always clear,
said the wind. I'm sorry.
You're saying I hold my hands
gingerly around the world
like a waist. No, not at all,
the mouth said. I'm saying
I don't think you're gentle at all.

*

The dentist said, Here is a tooth.
Look how smart you are,
the bridge said, patting his head.
Sometimes a tooth spends
its whole life inside
the mouth. I'm not so smart,
the dentist said. The mouth is
a field full of holes. Oh,
said the wind—no. No, it's not.

Robert Creeley Watching the Polls

He thinks these
days what isn't
a religion?   Why
is this question different

from all other
questions?   A referendum

If I were looking
for work

now   I would be a process
server   It's going
to be a long night
for months

Moonlighting

It turns out you cannot see
a better subject: the illumination
of a complimentary effort under
the cover of, if not darkness,
an appearing absence of light.

It's simpler to just look at the diamond
and accept how it was made, your focus
fully absorbed in the moment
of a task parallel to the point:

compress to skin before the suture,
a sleight of speech you must hear once
more to know how it will change

the evening's final course,
& your ear for it, that half-moon hung
askance above the tip of your tongue.

The Wish

The wish to be pregnant arrives inside a very old man.
I wish to be pregnant, he says to his wife.
You don't have the stomach for it, his wife says.

The next day the old man visits his doctor: *The wish to be pregnant has arrived inside me.*
A common lament in the end, the doctor says.

The very old man visits a pharmacy and buys a test.
I don't believe it, his wife says.

Months later, the old man is very pregnant.
He looks in the mirror toward what's arriving inside him.
What am I going to do with you, he says, *as the shape inside him grows.*

But there's nowhere for you to go, says the old man, as the shape inside him grows…

Tanka

The gulls lease their home
from the power company.
Beneath them, you try

to impregnate the sand, wind
knocking the wind out of you.

A Hue of the Sea

He held the egg in the nest of his hands
until it was winter, everything having turned the color
of a beach in the sun and back again as the egg grew
around his fingers, his knuckles cracking against
the thickening shell, turning blue and back again
into the black hue of the sea. He took his mouth
and asked his wife for water, which she poured into a vase
and carried back from the kitchen and into the living
room where he had sat to rest. He took a sip
and the egg grew over his wrists as she held the water
to his lips. He took another and lay back, letting the water
down his chin and over the egg onto the rug,
drop after drop, where new eggs grew, one after another
until his wife's legs reached like roots back to the sea.

A Diamond in the Universe
a translation for Jack Spicer

A howl of hairless dogs screams from the branches.

A dog killed the moon.

A howl of hairless dogs scream.

A seagull eyes the womb.

An Atrium as Aside the Sea

You sit in the lobby waiting for one thing
to become another thing, one moment
another moment, a time expecting to become
overcome, overrun by itself, when from inside your hands
you hear a siren. You lift your hands, hold them
up against your ears to hear the sea
behind the siren, which continues ringing
softly as you look about the lobby
to see if anyone is hearing what you hear,
the sea pitching softly as if against white sand,
the steady pitch of the siren pulsing
between the stained-glass windows
of your eyes, your breath a breeze escaping
below the snail shell of your mind, curling across
your lips & into the lobby, which you leave,
walking out into the spring where you lower your hands
from your ears to let the siren slip like a silk sheet
over the skin of the fountain you enter
as your head sings & your head sings
& the water rushes in.

Ballad of the Terrible Presence

a translation for Jack Spicer

I was eating lunch during wartime.
The wind was getting lost in the river,

and beside it the bull created a little shadow
by shitting in the grass. I was thinking about suffering.

Green poison collected. Elsewhere
cold meat kept being pressed into shapes

and prepped to ship off
to my hometown where I would take
its package from a brown paper bag
as a soldier sat beside a black cactus

and later that evening remembered
a little shadow across the distance.

The Little Halfwit

a translation for Jack Spicer

It wasn't late
but was after
noon & leaving.

It left a use-
less little
shrug.

A statue
played with
what remained.

Shadow of
the other fruits,
none stayed

clothed. Time is
only, was a joke.

I Wish Like Certain Fishes

Inside of ourselves is a shield that is possible
to maintain like a distinction between certain
wars and the world we hear about which
can never be addressed. Goals are running
back to us, an example of how not to fall
like a whip into the air. If you think about it
the answer is any number of things.
So far away from me the world continues.
I lie like a fish in my bed, such comfort blue
and moving through me. There ought to be rules.
In large part our enemies are any number of things.
I am a coyote. Desire and possibility. Technology.
These principles themselves don't leave us alone.

A Title That Comes from Their Sleep by the Clusters

a translation for Jack Spicer

While playing with the moon in the corner during the fight against terrorism
pulleys appear despite the obstacle of the sky.

The dead make their arrests.

You know you are capable, if you want
to move your desire,
or read before you decide to have children.

One Country May Hide Another

One country may hide another country idling inside it like a locomotive in the mountains, a surveyor peering from a distance above the humming cars, searching for signs of how or when you might return, for the manner of the field turning between the mountains, the country a quilt knitting across itself, the surveyor adjusting his tripod and level, his bright vest signaling that he is, after all, a part of the country he's looking both from and into. And you are, too. You know this,

though you know neither how he arrived, nor you. You wonder after his home, wonder why he left, why he stopped so near or was sent just past the foothills, which don't to you seem like warnings of anything; you wonder how he moved into the mountains, the country proud of its countryside and how it brims with life—though life, of course, is a warning of death, and death a warning of life, the trees a warning to the sky that the ground is reaching up like a child holding

a wand it waves at the mobile of planets spinning in the sky low above its head. Inside the child's head the bones shift slowly as plates inside the earth, which shakes each time the locomotive's engine prattles absent its forward motion. In the sleeping car you see a man talking to a grandmotherly woman holding her bag in her lap, her white gloves spotless despite the heat. Behind her you can see the boy playing jacks, though they've so long been out of fashion you wonder how he came

to find them. By chance, you imagine. And you suppose it's not by chance that he only has one eye, blue in its socket like a planet, and there must be a story to this. You know it. You want to ask his mother, though she is absent, the boy letting the ball fall off the pullout table he was playing on before sliding it back up upon itself and pushing it out of sight as he pushes slowly onward toward sleep. One dream may hide another dream. One dream may hide another country and its methods,

and from where you sit, the weather picking up over the peaks, pressing its white breath into the ground, deer running past the locomotive as it lays there laboring through such restless sleep, you can only believe in the mountains, the wind, the warm breath of laboring underneath the snow. When it melts, you know, the ground will seem to rise, just as steam rises above the locomotive, the surveyor barely noticing it now as he looks over the landscape, the planet, hidden, as it is, at intervals, by what's inside it.

Our Chef Is Delicious

When we first found him,

he was a poor creature who couldn't handle a paring knife,
             but that year in Tuscany did him well.

He returned a devout palate.

A man of peculiar desire.
             Please note, he must be garnished with mint;

                          chop finely, so, when rare, the meat bathes
                          the cut leaf.

It was a long day when our chef committed himself
             to the fineries of flesh—

                          the first drop of blood crowned the shaved
                          Parmesan;

the bouillabaisse thickened.
             Loving the body for the body alone is bitter.

                          He knew this, yes. He always thought parsley

the sprig of amateurs. At high temperatures
             his flesh will emit a faint, distinguished odor,

but this is common

for roasts of his nature. Add Chianti just after the boil.
    That his lips were cracked with salt is no cause for concern—

        thirst is

the first measure of longing.
        Open this. Breathe a short while before we eat.

Acknowledgments

Thank you to the editors of the publications where many of these poems first appeared, sometimes under different titles.

AGNI: "An Economics"
AGNI Online: "Instructional Ghazal"
Always Crashing: "A Diamond in the Universe," "A Language or Barrier of Love," "Tanka," "The Little Halfwit"
Artifice Magazine: "The Book of Echoes" (as "Ars Poetica, a Cento")
Cincinnati Review: "Reservoirs"
Conduit: "Georges Gilles de la Tourette"
Copper Nickel: "A Hue of the Sea," "Ventriloquy"
Court Green: "The Ladder"
Gulf Coast: "Nevermind the Lightning," "Study for Two Swans"
Indiana Review: "An Atrium as Aside the Sea" (as "The Present Tense")
Memorious: "One Country May Hide Another," "Prodrome" (as "Year of the Goat")
Meridian: "Self-Portrait as Horizon"
Mississippi Review: "Ballad of the Terrible Presence"
New Orleans Review: "Variations on a Theme by Breton"
Pleiades: "Echopraxia," "Our Chef Is Delicious," "Tourette Syndrome," "Tourette's as Thanks for Everything You Can Put in Your Mouth"
Quarterly West: "I Doubt They Would Notice the Mustachioed Man's Wife," "You Meet Someone and Later You Meet Their Dancing and You Have to Start Again"
Sixth Finch: "Postscript for the Beginning"
SPORK: "As for Names"
Sprung Formal: "Frog," "Passages," "Robert Creeley Watching the Polls"
Third Coast: "Reverse Ghazal"
TriQuarterly Online: "Upper Peninsula," "What's It To You"

TYPO: "I Wish Like Certain Fishes"
VOLT: "A Title That Comes from Their Sleep by the Clusters"

"Georges Gilles de la Tourette" appeared as the *Verse Daily* poem of the day on April 15, 2020.

"I Doubt They Would Notice the Mustachioed Man's Wife" & "You Meet Someone and Later You Meet Their Dancing and You Have to Start Again" are reprinted on *poets.org*.

"Wild Asparagus" received the 2014 Lucille Medwick Memorial Award from the Poetry Society of America & was first published on *poetrysociety.org*. Thank you to Jericho Brown for the selection.

Thank you to all who encouraged me while I wrote these poems, especially Nik De Dominic, Jeremy Allan Hawkins, & Avni Vyas.

Thank you to Kyle Churney, Matt Kelsey, Kenyatta Rogers, & Jacob Saenz for community & camaraderie.

Thank you to Jennifer Harris, Simone Muench, & Richard Siken for believing in this book.

Thank you to my family, Laura Anne Welch, Greg Welch, & Kathy Curtis, for the unwavering support.

For love & joy, thank you to Justine Houghton.

Notes

"The Book of Echoes" is a cento composed of lines, in order, from each poem in Ted Berrigan's *The Sonnets.*

"Echolalia" is a cento composed of lines and fragments by: Linda Bierds, Kathy Fagan, Neil Fischer, Sasha Pimentel, Kenneth Patchen, Walt Whitman, Anna Swir, Alberto Ríos, Louis Simpson, Nickole Brown, Sara Teasdale, & Charles Bernstein.

"A Language or Barrier of Love," "Passages," "Postscript for the Beginning," "Frog," "A Diamond in the Universe," "Ballad of the Terrible Presence," "The Little Halfwit," & "A Title That Comes from Their Sleep by the Clusters" are English-to-English translations of poems from Jack Spicer's *After Lorca.*

Additional poems throughout the book adopt lines or gestures from the following poets:

"Tourette's as Thanks for Everything You Can Put in Your Mouth": Su Cho

"Tourette Syndrome": Ko Un

"Variations on a Theme by Breton": André Breton

"Tourette's as Bildungsroman": Frank Bidart

"Self-Portrait as Horizon": Hayden Carruth

"You Meet Someone and Later You Meet Their Dancing and You Have to Start Again": Heather Christle

"Dear Hell": Arthur Rimbaud

"Cesarean": Nicole Sealey

"Reservoirs": Agha Shahid Ali

"Reverse Ghazal": Heather McHugh

"I Doubt They Would Notice the Mustachioed Man's Wife": John Ashbery

"I Wish Like Certain Fishes": CD Wright

"One Country May Hide Another": Kenneth Koch

"Nevermind the Lighting": James Tate

"The Course of Human History Personified" takes its title from an art book by Marcel Dzama, who took the title from Dante. The poem is for Richard Siken.

About the Author

David Gregory Welch is the author of *Everyone Who Is Dead* (Spork Press, 2018) and a chapbook, *It Is Such a Good Thing to Be In Love With You* (The Laurel Review/Midwest Chapbook Series, 2015). He is the recipient of awards from the Academy of American Poets, the Poetry Society of America, and the Sewanee Writers' Conference. Welch lives in Chicago and teaches occasionally at DePaul University and StoryStudio Chicago.

JACKLEG PRESS

V. Joshua Adams * Mark Baumgartner * Scott Shibuya Brown * Michael Chin * Chloe Clark * Rivka Clifton * Brittney Corrigan * Jessica Cuello * Barbara Cully * Allison Cundiff * Curious Theatre Branch * Genevieve DeGuzman * Suzanne Frischkorn * Victoria Garza * Reginald Gibbons * Joachim Glage * Caroline Goodwin * Brett Hanley * Summer Hart * Kathryn Kruse * Brigitte Lewis * Jenny Magnus * DK McCutchen * Rita Mookerjee * Mamie Morgan * Alexis Orgera * Zach Powers * Karen Rigby * Jo Salas * Maureen Seaton * Kristine Snodgrass * Cornelia Spelman * Peter Stenson * Melissa Studdard * Gemini Wahhaj * Megan Weiler * David Gregory Welch * Cassandra Whitaker * David Wesley Williams

jacklegpress.org

www.ingramcontent.com/pod-product-compliance
Lightning Source LLC
Chambersburg PA
CBHW041146120626
46547CB00020B/3132